PREDATOR
SPLASHDOWN

26 FEARSOME BATTLES:
From the shallows to the deep

BY PAUL BECK

SCHOLASTIC

Published by Tangerine Press, an imprint of Scholastic Inc.,
557 Broadway, New York, NY 10012
Scholastic Canada Ltd., Markham, Ontario
Scholastic New Zealand Ltd., Greenmount, Auckland
Scholastic Australia Pty. Ltd., Gosford NSW
Grolier International, Inc., Makati City, Philippines
Scholastic UK, Coventry, Warwickshire

an imprint of
SCHOLASTIC
www.scholastic.com

Produced by becker&mayer!, LLC.
11120 NE 33rd Place, Suite 101,
Bellevue, WA 98004
www.beckermayer.com

becker&mayer!
BOOK PRODUCERS

If you have questions or comments about this product, please visit www.beckermayer.com/customerservice.html and click on the Customer Service Request Form.

Author: Paul Beck
Designer: Rosanna Brockley
Editor: Ruth Austin
Photo researcher: Donna Metcalf
Production coordinator: Cindy Curren

Image Credits
Front cover: © PHOTOCREO Michal Bednarak/Shutterstock; © jeffreychin/Shutterstock; © Minden Pictures/SuperStock; Front/back cover: © Romolo Tavani/Shutterstock. Page 6: © Ethan Daniels/Shutterstock. Page 7: © Auscape/UIG/agefotostock. Page 8: © Tony Arruza/Getty Images. Page 9: © Minden Pictures/SuperStock. Page 10: © Yusran Adbul Rahman/Shutterstock. Page 11: Rich Carey/Shutterstock. Page 12: © MISCELLANEOUSTOCK/Alamy. Page 13: © Dan Exton/Shutterstock. Page 14: © Biosphoto/SuperStock. Page 15: © SeaPics.com. Page 16: Mikhail Blajenov/Dreamstime. Page 17: © Moelyn Photos/Getty Images. Page 18: aquapix/Shutterstock. Page 19: Anky10/Dreamstime. Page 20: © Westend61/SuperStock. Page 21: © Seapics.com. Page 22: © Dante Fenolio/Getty Images; © SeaPics.com. Page 23: © Minden Pictures/SuperStock; © Norbert Wu/Minden Pictures/National Geographic Creative; © Dustie/Shutterstock; © Dante Fenolio/Science Source. Pages 22–23: © Andrew Kuzim/Shutterstock. Page 24: © Juniors Bildarchiv GmbH/Alamy. Page 25: © Stefan Pircher/Shutterstock. Page 26: © Richard Wear/agefotostock. Page 27: © Radius Images/Corbis. Page 28: © Beth Swanson/Shutterstock. Page 29: © Joe Quinn/Shutterstock. Page 30: © Stephen Frink/Getty Images. Page 31: © David Doubilet/Getty Images. Page 32: © Thomas Haider/Getty Images. Page 33: © Brian J. Skerry/National Geographic Creative. Page 34: © Howard Chew/Dreamstime; © Maxim Khytra/Shutterstock; © Cigdem Sean Cooper/Shutterstock. Pages 34–35: © Stephen Kerkhofs/Shutterstock. Page 35: © Willyem Bradberry/Shutterstock; © Visuals Unlimited, Inc./David Fleetham/Getty Images; © Mirage3/Dreamstime. Page 36: © Helmut Corneli/imageb/imageBROKER/SuperStock. Page 37: © Norbert Wu/Getty Images. Page 38: © Mark Conlin/Getty Images. Page 39: Awashima Marine Park/Getty Images. Page 40: © Jason Edwards/National Geographic Creative. Page 41: © Stephen Alvarez/Getty Images. Page 42: © Richard Setire/Getty Images. Page 43: Marek Velechovsky/Shutterstock. Page 44: © Bluehand/Dreamstime. Page 45: © Michael Durham/Getty Images. Page 46: © Gerald A. DeBoer/Shutterstock. Page 47: © Lukas Blazek/Dreamstime. Page 48: Amazon-Images/Alamy. Page 49: Redmond Durrell/Alamy. Page 50: © Spilogics/Dreamstime; © Ryan M. Bolton/Shutterstock; © prochasson Frederic/Dreamstime. Pages 50–51: © Scubaluna/Shutterstock. Page 51: © worldwildlifewonders/Shutterstock; © NHPA/SuperStock; © reptiles4all/Shutterstock. Page 52: © Papilio/Alamy. Page 53: © Arco Images GmbH/Alamy. Page 54: © Gerard Lacz Images/SuperStock. Page 55: © Cyril Ruoso/Minden Pictures/Getty Images. Page 56: Todd Gustafson/Panora/agefotostock. Page 57: © Steve Allen/Getty Images. Page 58: © Dave Watts/Alamy. Page 59: © Andrey Neskrasov/Alamy. Page 60: © Rich Carey/Shutterstock. Page 61: © Rafael Ben-Ari/Alamy. Page 62: © imageBROKER/SuperStock. Page 63: © imageBROKER/Alamy. Design elements used throughout: © remart/Shutterstock, © remart/Shutterstock; © Shutterstock/StudioSmart, © Designstock/Shutterstock, © siro46/Shutterstock.

Printed, manufactured, and assembled in Jefferson City, Missouri, USA, June 2015

10 9 8 7 6 5 4 3 2 1
ISBN: 978-0-545-86453-4
15017

Massive jaws. Venomous barbs. Electric jolts. Underwater predators have a store of weapons that give them the advantage over their prey. But what would happen if you pitted these predators against one another?

A WATER WORLD

HUDSON BAY

Missouri River

THE GREAT LAKES

Mississippi River

PACIFIC OCEAN

ATLANTIC OCEAN

Amazon River

We live in a water world. Water covers more than 70 percent of Earth's surface. Water-dwelling animals (and plants, too!) can be divided into two main habitats: salt water and fresh water.

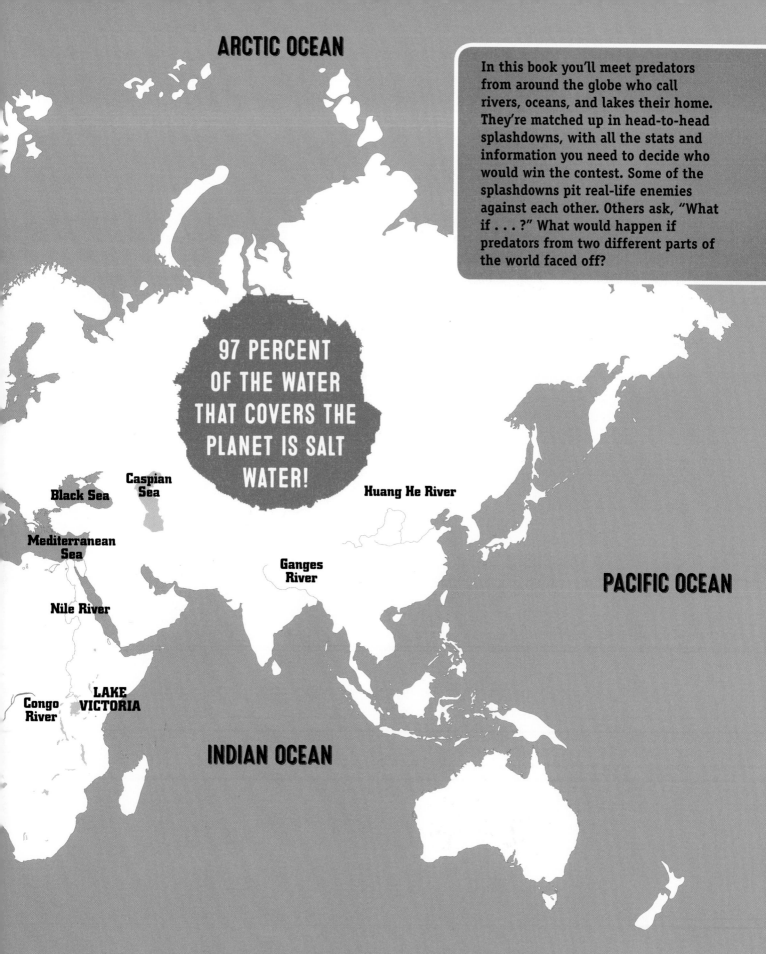

ARCTIC OCEAN

In this book you'll meet predators from around the globe who call rivers, oceans, and lakes their home. They're matched up in head-to-head splashdowns, with all the stats and information you need to decide who would win the contest. Some of the splashdowns pit real-life enemies against each other. Others ask, "What if . . . ?" What would happen if predators from two different parts of the world faced off?

97 PERCENT OF THE WATER THAT COVERS THE PLANET IS SALT WATER!

Black Sea

Caspian Sea

Huang He River

Mediterranean Sea

Ganges River

PACIFIC OCEAN

Nile River

Congo River

LAKE VICTORIA

INDIAN OCEAN

SOUTHERN OCEAN

BANDED SEA KRAIT VS. SEA SNAKE

BANDED SEA KRAIT

This snake hunts eels in the crevices of coral reefs. With its round body and paddle-like tail, it's equally at home on land and in the water.

SCIENTIFIC NAME	*Laticauda colubrina*
LENGTH	2.5–4 feet (76–122 cm)
TYPICAL PREY	Eels
PREDATOR STYLE	Hunts eels in coral reefs; subdues them with its venomous bite
WATER TYPE	Salt

STATS

SPEED	4
STRENGTH	4
BRAINS	4
ATTACK	7
DEFENSE	7

THE SPLASHDOWN

A head-to-head match between two venomous seagoing snakes! The banded sea krait hunts and feeds in water but goes on land to rest, nest, and lay eggs. The yellow-bellied sea snake spends its entire life at sea.

YELLOW-BELLIED SEA SNAKE

This snake can stay under water for up to three hours. Its narrow flattened body makes it an expert swimmer, but it can't crawl on land.

STATS

4	SPEED	
4	STRENGTH	
4	BRAINS	
7	ATTACK	
7	DEFENSE	

SCIENTIFIC NAME	*Pelamis platurus*
LENGTH	1–3.5 feet (30–107 cm)
TYPICAL PREY	Fish
PREDATOR STYLE	Floats on the surface to ambush fish as they swim up underneath
WATER TYPE	Salt

WHO WINS? SEE PAGE 64.

BLUE MARLIN VS. SWORDFISH

BLUE MARLIN

Famous as a fighter, the blue marlin is the biggest of the billfishes. Large females can weigh in at nearly 1 ton (900 kg).

SCIENTIFIC NAME	*Makaira nigricans*
LENGTH	7–16 feet (2.1–4.9 m)
TYPICAL PREY	Open-ocean fish such as tuna, mackerel, and dolphinfish (mahi-mahi)
PREDATOR STYLE	Swims right into schools of fish to attack, may stun prey with quick sideways slashes of its bill
WATER TYPE	Salt

STATS

SPEED	10
STRENGTH	9
BRAINS	6
ATTACK	7
DEFENSE	8

THE SPLASHDOWN

This splashdown pits two powerful members of the billfish family against each other. These open-ocean predators may look as if they're about to cross swords, but they don't use these bills as stabbing weapons. The bill is an extension of the upper jaw.

SWORDFISH

Swordfish can dive deeper than 2,000 feet (610 m) in pursuit of prey. This fish is one of the fastest swimmers in the ocean.

STATS

10	SPEED
9	STRENGTH
6	BRAINS
7	ATTACK
7	DEFENSE

SCIENTIFIC NAME	*Xiphias gladius*
LENGTH	5–14.5 feet (1.5–4.4 m)
TYPICAL PREY	Open-ocean fish of all types, sometimes squid or cuttlefish
PREDATOR STYLE	Slashes with its bill to stun, kill, or knock prey out of a school of fish
WATER TYPE	Salt

WHO WINS? SEE PAGE 64.

LESSER BLUE-RINGED OCTOPUS

This pint-sized predator displays its bright blue rings when threatened or alarmed. It produces two types of venom: one for prey and one for defense.

SCIENTIFIC NAME	*Hapalochlaena maculosa*
LENGTH	Up to 8 inches (20 cm) total length, including arms. Its mantle (head) is 2.5 inches (6 cm)
TYPICAL PREY	Crabs and shrimp
PREDATOR STYLE	Bites or spits its venom into the water around prey—scientists aren't sure
WATER TYPE	Salt

STATS

SPEED	5
STRENGTH	4
BRAINS	7
ATTACK	7
DEFENSE	10

THE SPLASHDOWN

The world's most venomous mollusk and most venomous fish square off in a coral-reef battle. These predators may be small, but their self-defense toxins can be deadly to humans and large animals. Only the octopus uses its venom for hunting.

REEF STONEFISH

This camouflaged fish blends in perfectly with the rocks and coral where it lives. The 13 venomous spines on its back are strictly for defense.

STATS

3	SPEED	
3	STRENGTH	
3	BRAINS	
2	ATTACK	
10	DEFENSE	

SCIENTIFIC NAME	*Synanceia verrucosa*
LENGTH	10–15 inches (25–38 cm)
TYPICAL PREY	Small fish and crustaceans such as crabs
PREDATOR STYLE	Waits in ambush, then gulps down prey when it swims in range
WATER TYPE	Salt

WHO WINS?
SEE PAGE 64.

BLUEFIN TUNA VS. LIONFISH

ATLANTIC BLUEFIN TUNA

These huge, fast-swimming fish travel long distances across the ocean in schools. Unlike most fish, they are endothermic (warm-blooded) and create their own body heat.

SCIENTIFIC NAME	*Thunnus thynnus*
LENGTH	6–9.75 feet (1.8–3 m)
TYPICAL PREY	Smaller fish of all types, squid, and crustaceans
PREDATOR STYLE	Sprints with bursts of speed to chase fast schools of fish; cruises along with its mouth open to gulp down slower-moving prey
WATER TYPE	Salt

STATS

SPEED	10
STRENGTH	8
BRAINS	5
ATTACK	5
DEFENSE	5

THE SPLASHDOWN

What if . . . ? These two predators will probably never meet in the real world, but with the invasive lionfish spreading through North American waters, it's not impossible. Can the lionfish's venomous spines stand up to the tuna's vastly superior size?

RED LIONFISH

The venomous spines on this fish's back are for defense, not hunting. But lionfish are aggressive and may threaten or attack with their spines facing forward.

STATS

3	SPEED	
3	STRENGTH	
3	BRAINS	
3	ATTACK	
9	DEFENSE	

SCIENTIFIC NAME	*Pterois volitans*
LENGTH	12–15 inches (30–38 cm)
TYPICAL PREY	Crabs, shrimp, and small fish
PREDATOR STYLE	Stalks, then strikes when the prey is cornered and swallows it whole
WATER TYPE	Salt

WHO WINS? SEE PAGE 64.

NORTHERN STARGAZER

The stargazer's upward-staring eyes let it watch for prey while buried in the sand. This fish defends itself with an electric shock of up to 50 volts.

SCIENTIFIC NAME	*Astroscopus guttatus*
LENGTH	8–22 inches (20–56 cm)
TYPICAL PREY	Any small fish that swim close enough
PREDATOR STYLE	Hides under the sand, then pops up to swallow prey whole
WATER TYPE	Salt

STATS

SPEED	2
STRENGTH	2
BRAINS	3
ATTACK	3
DEFENSE	5

THE SPLASHDOWN

What if . . . ? East meets west as two ocean-bottom predators try to out-zap each other in this electrifying contest. The stargazer and electric ray live on opposite coasts of North America. Both predators can zing their enemies with an electric shock.

PACIFIC ELECTRIC RAY

This electrifying predator can zap an attacker with a 50-volt jolt, enough to knock a human down. It also uses its electricity to subdue prey.

STATS	
4	SPEED
4	STRENGTH
4	BRAINS
5	ATTACK
5	DEFENSE

SCIENTIFIC NAME	*Torpedo californica*
LENGTH	2–4.5 feet (61–137 cm)
TYPICAL PREY	Fish
PREDATOR STYLE	Hunts by swimming in the water column at night and by ambush on the sea floor during the day; subdues prey with electric shocks
WATER TYPE	Salt

WHO WINS?
SEE PAGE 64.

GIANT PACIFIC OCTOPUS

This giant is a master of camouflage, changing color to blend in with its surroundings. Its soft body also lets it squeeze into very small hiding places.

SCIENTIFIC NAME	*Enteroctopus dofleini*
LENGTH	9–16 feet (2.7–4.9 m)
TYPICAL PREY	Crabs, clams, snails, fish, and anything else it can catch
PREDATOR STYLE	Waits in ambush, then grabs prey with sucker-covered arms and paralyzes it with a venomous bite
WATER TYPE	Salt

STATS

SPEED	5
STRENGTH	8
BRAINS	9
ATTACK	6
DEFENSE	6

THE SPLASHDOWN

It's mollusk against mammal as the world's largest octopus meets the swift-swimming harbor seal. Octopuses are sometimes on the seal's dinner menu, but this one's a bit different: its arms can spread wider than the length of a minivan!

HARBOR SEAL

This hunter can hold its breath for more than 20 minutes and dive as deep as 650 feet (198 m), but most hunting dives are shorter and shallower.

STATS

7	SPEED
7	STRENGTH
8	BRAINS
6	ATTACK
6	DEFENSE

SCIENTIFIC NAME	*Phoca vitulina*
LENGTH	5–6 feet (1.5–1.8 m)
TYPICAL PREY	Fish, octopuses, squid, crabs, and shrimp
PREDATOR STYLE	Chases schools of fish, dives to sea bottom for octopuses, crabs, and shrimp
WATER TYPE	Salt

WHO WINS?
SEE PAGE 64.

GREAT BARRACUDA

The torpedo-shaped predator has two separate sets of razor-sharp teeth. It rams into large prey with its jaws open and chomps the fish into pieces.

SCIENTIFIC NAME	*Sphyraena barracuda*
LENGTH	3–6 feet (91–183 cm)
TYPICAL PREY	Fish
PREDATOR STYLE	Hunts by sight and speed
WATER TYPE	Salt

STATS

SPEED	9
STRENGTH	6
BRAINS	5
ATTACK	7
DEFENSE	6

THE SPLASHDOWN

Two top predators face off in this coral-reef splashdown. The great barracuda is built for speed, with a slim body and a mouth bristling with pointy teeth. The gray reef shark is one of the most aggressive shark species.

GRAY REEF SHARK

The gray reef shark lives in coral reef areas of the Pacific and Indian Oceans. This aggressive shark has been known to attack humans.

STATS

8	SPEED	
8	STRENGTH	
	5	BRAINS
8	ATTACK	
8	DEFENSE	

SCIENTIFIC NAME	*Carcharhinus amblyrhynchos*
LENGTH	4–8 feet (1.2–2.4 m)
TYPICAL PREY	Fish, sometimes including other gray reef sharks; also squid, octopuses, crabs, and shrimp
PREDATOR STYLE	Prowls for prey near coral reefs, most often at night
WATER TYPE	Salt

WHO WINS?
SEE PAGE 64.

GREAT HAMMERHEAD VS. LEMON SHARK

GREAT HAMMERHEAD SHARK

Like other sharks, the great hammerhead has electricity-sensing organs in its head for detecting prey. The wide head shape spreads these organs out for better sensitivity.

SCIENTIFIC NAME	*Sphyrna mokarran*
LENGTH	10–20 feet (3–6.1 m)
TYPICAL PREY	Fish, especially rays and skates
PREDATOR STYLE	Hunts along the sea floor using special electricity-sensing organs to detect stingrays and other bottom fish
WATER TYPE	Salt

STATS

SPEED	7
STRENGTH	9
BRAINS	5
ATTACK	9
DEFENSE	9

THE SPLASHDOWN

The largest of the hammerhead sharks, the great hammerhead sometimes preys on young lemon sharks. But at more than 10 feet (3 m) long, a full-grown lemon shark is a different story. Who will prove toughest in this shark-to-shark splashdown?

LEMON SHARK

This shark gets its name from its yellow-brown color. Lemon sharks live in coastal waters of North and South America, as well as West Africa.

STATS

7	SPEED
9	STRENGTH
5	BRAINS
8	ATTACK
8	DEFENSE

SCIENTIFIC NAME	*Negaprion brevirostris*
LENGTH	8–11 feet (2.4–3.4 m)
TYPICAL PREY	Fish, crabs, crayfish, sometimes seabirds
PREDATOR STYLE	Stalks prey near the sea floor in shallow areas
WATER TYPE	Salt

WHO WINS?
SEE PAGE 64.

BELOW THE SURFACE:
INTO THE DEEP

In the salty habitat of the ocean, the animals, plants, and other life-forms live in different zones.

One way of dividing up the life zones is based on how close the habitat is to shore. Another is based on whether the animals live at the surface, on the sea floor, or in the water column (all the water between the surface and the bottom). Still another is based on how deep the water is and how much light reaches there.

The deep zone, reached by only 1 percent of sunlight or less, is called the aphotic zone. It starts at a depth of about 650 feet (198 m) and goes all the way to the deepest bottom of the ocean.

These are just some of the special weapons used by splashdown predators who live or hunt in the aphotic zone:

GIANT MOUTH

ANGLERFISH

FRILLED SHARK

LURE ON HEAD

ANGLERFISH

LURE ON CHIN

PACIFIC BLACKDRAGON

TRIPLE-SPIKED TEETH

PACIFIC BLACKDRAGON

TENTACLES

GIANT OCTOPUS

ORCA VS. GREAT WHITE SHARK

ORCA

Orcas, or killer whales, live and hunt together in groups called pods. They live in more parts of the world than any other marine mammal.

SCIENTIFIC NAME	*Orcinus orca*
LENGTH	20–32 feet (6.1–9.8 m)
TYPICAL PREY	Fish, seals, sea lions, porpoises, smaller whales
PREDATOR STYLE	Pack hunter; uses echolocation (sonar) to find and pursue prey
WATER TYPE	Salt

STATS

SPEED	9
STRENGTH	10
BRAINS	9
ATTACK	10
DEFENSE	10

THE SPLASHDOWN

It's an epic battle between the ocean's apex predators! Orcas are the biggest members of the dolphin family, with males weighing as much as 11 tons (10,000 kg). The great white shark is the world's biggest predatory fish.

GREAT WHITE SHARK

This shark usually swims just under the surface, then attacks with a rush from below. One razor-toothed bite can cut through flesh, bone, and even turtle shells.

STATS

7	SPEED	
10	STRENGTH	
5	BRAINS	
10	ATTACK	
10	DEFENSE	

SCIENTIFIC NAME	*Carcharodon carcharias*
LENGTH	14–20 feet (4.3–6.1 m)
TYPICAL PREY	Seals, sea lions, dolphins, large fish
PREDATOR STYLE	Attacks with a surprise rush from below
WATER TYPE	Salt

WHO WINS?
SEE PAGE 64.

POLAR BEAR VS. WALRUS

POLAR BEAR

The polar bear is the largest land predator, but it does all of its hunting in or around the ocean. Its scientific name means "sea bear."

SCIENTIFIC NAME	*Ursus maritimus*
LENGTH	6.5–8.5 feet (2–2.6 m)
TYPICAL PREY	Seals, walruses, small whales, birds, carrion, plants
PREDATOR STYLE	Waits at ice edge to ambush surfacing seals; stalks hauled-out seals from the ice or swims up from underwater for a surprise attack
WATER TYPE	Salt

STATS

SPEED	7
STRENGTH	10
BRAINS	8
ATTACK	10
DEFENSE	10

THE SPLASHDOWN

Two old enemies meet in an arctic splashdown! Polar bears will prey on young walruses, but a full-grown adult is another matter. These huge relatives of seals and sea lions come equipped with long tusks and can weigh more than 1 ton (900 kg).

WALRUS

Both male and female walruses have tusks. Males will use their tusks as weapons to defend territory and to protect harems of females during mating season.

STATS		
8	SPEED	
8	STRENGTH	
8	BRAINS	
6	ATTACK	
7	DEFENSE	

SCIENTIFIC NAME	*Odobenus rosmarus*
LENGTH	7–11 feet (2.1–3.4 m)
TYPICAL PREY	Clams, mussels, crabs, worms, snails, and other ocean-floor invertebrates
PREDATOR STYLE	Dives to the ocean floor, feels with its whiskers along the bottom to locate prey in murky water
WATER TYPE	Salt

WHO WINS?
SEE PAGE 64.

BALLOONFISH VS. OYSTER TOADFISH

BALLOONFISH

When threatened, this fish inflates itself with water until it is almost completely spherical. Sharp spines stick out of its body to keep attackers at bay.

SCIENTIFIC NAME	*Diodon holocanthus*
LENGTH	8–20 inches (20–51 cm)
TYPICAL PREY	Snails, sea urchins, hermit crabs
PREDATOR STYLE	Hunts at night along the ocean floor
WATER TYPE	Salt

STATS

SPEED	3
STRENGTH	2
BRAINS	4
ATTACK	1
DEFENSE	6

THE SPLASHDOWN

The prickly balloonfish meets the warty-looking toadfish in a contest of shell-crunching mollusk-eaters. Both of these bottom dwellers subdue their prey with powerful jaws and crushing teeth. But can the toadfish get past the balloonfish's prickly spines?

OYSTER TOADFISH

This fish defends itself with snapping jaws and a spiny dorsal (back) fin. During mating season, males call to females with a booming, foghorn-like voice.

STATS

3	SPEED	
3	STRENGTH	
3	BRAINS	
2	ATTACK	
9	DEFENSE	

SCIENTIFIC NAME	*Opsanus tau*
LENGTH	Up to 12 inches (30 cm)
TYPICAL PREY	Mollusks, crustaceans, small fish, squid
PREDATOR STYLE	Snaps up prey with its powerful jaws
WATER TYPE	Salt

WHO WINS?
SEE PAGE 64.

PORTUGUESE MAN-OF-WAR VS. AUSTRALIAN BOX JELLYFISH

PORTUGUESE MAN-OF-WAR

This "predator" is made up of individual, smaller animals called polyps. Four different types of polyps form the float, tendrils, and digestive and reproductive systems.

SCIENTIFIC NAME	*Physalia physalis*
LENGTH	Its float is only 12 inches (30 cm), but its tendrils can extend 30–165 feet (9–50 m)
TYPICAL PREY	Small fish and fish larvae, squid
PREDATOR STYLE	Drifts with wind and current, stings prey that gets caught in its tendrils
WATER TYPE	Salt

STATS

SPEED	1
STRENGTH	1
BRAINS	1
ATTACK	8
DEFENSE	8

THE SPLASHDOWN

Two venomous predators go tentacle-to-tentacle in this contest. The Portuguese man-of-war is actually a colony of animals that join together to form a jellyfish-like structure. The box jellyfish is a single, deadly animal. Both hunt by stinging their prey with powerful toxins.

AUSTRALIAN BOX JELLYFISH

This box jellyfish is one of the deadliest animals in the world. Its tentacles sting with powerful venom that can be fatal to even large animals and humans.

STATS

1	SPEED
1	STRENGTH
1	BRAINS
10	ATTACK
10	DEFENSE

SCIENTIFIC NAME	*Chironex fleckeri*
LENGTH	Tentacles as long as 10 feet (3 m), with a 12-inch (30-cm) bell
TYPICAL PREY	Fish and shrimp
PREDATOR STYLE	Propels itself through the water, stings prey that gets caught in its tentacles
WATER TYPE	Salt

WHO WINS?
SEE PAGE 64.

SPERM WHALE VS. GIANT SQUID

SPERM WHALE

This bus-sized whale is the biggest toothed predator on Earth. Sperm whales can dive deeper than a mile (1.6 km) and hold their breath for an hour and a half.

SCIENTIFIC NAME	*Physeter macrocephalus*
LENGTH	25–50 feet (7.6–15.2 m)
TYPICAL PREY	Squid and octopuses
PREDATOR STYLE	Dives as deep as 0.6 miles (1 km) or more in pursuit of squid; probably uses echolocation (sonar) to find prey
WATER TYPE	Salt

STATS

SPEED	8
STRENGTH	10
BRAINS	8
ATTACK	8
DEFENSE	7

THE SPLASHDOWN

Ancient opponents face off far below the surface in this deep-sea splashdown. Sperm whales' favorite prey is squid, but the tentacle scars on many whales' heads are proof that the giant squid can hold its own in a fight.

GIANT SQUID

This deep-sea giant's basketball-sized eyes are the largest in the animal kingdom. Before 2004, no one had ever taken a picture of a living giant squid.

STATS

6	SPEED	
9	STRENGTH	
6	BRAINS	
8	ATTACK	
9	DEFENSE	

SCIENTIFIC NAME	*Architeuthis dux*
LENGTH	10–40 feet (3–12.2 m)
TYPICAL PREY	Deep sea fish, smaller squid
PREDATOR STYLE	Grabs prey with its two club-tipped tentacles, then drags it within reach of eight arms and a parrot-like beak
WATER TYPE	Salt

WHO WINS?
SEE PAGE 64.

BELOW THE SURFACE:
THE UPPER OCEAN

The ocean's upper life zone, where there is enough sunlight for plants and algae, is called the photic zone. This zone goes from the surface down to about 650 feet (168 m). Photic-zone predators include animals that live near the surface, in the water column, or on the sea bottom.

These are some of the special weapons used by splashdown predators who live or hunt at least some of the time in the photic zone:

VENOMOUS BITE

BANDED SEA KRAIT

VENOMOUS SPINES

LIONFISH

ELECTRIC SHOCK

ELECTRIC RAY

TEETH

GREAT WHITE SHARK

VENOMOUS STING

JELLYFISH

CLAWS

POLAR BEAR

HUMPBACK ANGLERFISH

Also known as the black seadevil, this deep-ocean dweller attracts prey to its doom with a glowing lure. The lure's blue glow comes from light-emitting bacteria.

SCIENTIFIC NAME	*Melanocetus johnsonii*
LENGTH	Up to 7 inches (18 cm)
TYPICAL PREY	Deep-sea fish
PREDATOR STYLE	Attracts prey with glowing lure at the end of its "fishing rod"
WATER TYPE	Salt

STATS

SPEED	2
STRENGTH	2
BRAINS	2
ATTACK	5
DEFENSE	5

THE SPLASHDOWN

Two bizarre-looking predators meet in the complete darkness of the deepest ocean. Both of these fish have bioluminescent (living, light-producing) organs that glow in the dark. These glowing lures attract prey in a world where animals are few and far between.

PELICAN EEL

This predator's huge mouth opens enough to gulp down prey wider than the eel itself. Its tail has a pink-glowing tip that may act as a lure.

STATS

2	SPEED	
2	STRENGTH	
2	BRAINS	
2	ATTACK	
2	DEFENSE	

SCIENTIFIC NAME	*Eurypharynx pelecanoides*
LENGTH	Up to 30 inches (76 cm)
TYPICAL PREY	Fish, crustaceans, squid
PREDATOR STYLE	Lunges and gulps prey down with its enormous mouth
WATER TYPE	Salt

WHO WINS?
SEE PAGE 64.

PACIFIC BLACKDRAGON

This deep-sea fish swims up to shallower waters at night to feed. Its long "chin whisker," called a barbel, may act as a lure to attract prey.

SCIENTIFIC NAME	*Idiacanthus antrostomus*
LENGTH	Up to 2 feet (61 cm)
TYPICAL PREY	Crustaceans and small fish
PREDATOR STYLE	Swims closer to the surface at night to feed, then returns to the lower depths during the day; may attract prey with its dangling lure
WATER TYPE	Salt

STATS

SPEED	2
STRENGTH	3
BRAINS	2
ATTACK	3
DEFENSE	3

THE SPLASHDOWN

This deep-sea splashdown may look like a mismatch between the fang-mouthed blackdragon and the much larger frilled shark, but size isn't everything. Speed counts, too, and the blackdragon may be faster. Scientists don't know much about these mysterious fishes' hunting behavior.

FRILLED SHARK

This deep-dwelling, eel-like shark has a mouth lined with hundreds of triple-spiked teeth. The multiple rows of teeth are good for grabbing and holding slippery squid.

STATS

6	SPEED	
5	STRENGTH	
3	BRAINS	
6	ATTACK	
6	DEFENSE	

SCIENTIFIC NAME	*Chlamydoselachus anguineus*
LENGTH	3–5 feet (91–152 cm)
TYPICAL PREY	Squid, fish, other sharks; may also eat carrion (dead animals) that drift down to the depths
PREDATOR STYLE	Slow swimmer, probably unable to chase fast-moving prey
WATER TYPE	Salt

WHO WINS?
SEE PAGE 64.

GREEN ANACONDA VS. ARAPAIMA

GREEN ANACONDA

Growing as long as a school bus and weighing up to a quarter of a ton (227 kg), the green anaconda is the biggest snake in the world.

SCIENTIFIC NAME	*Eunectes murinus*
LENGTH	20–30 feet (6.1–9.1 m)
TYPICAL PREY	Anything it can catch, including fish, amphibians, reptiles, birds, and mammals
PREDATOR STYLE	Ambush hunter; grabs prey with its teeth, then suffocates it by squeezing
WATER TYPE	Fresh

STATS

SPEED	6
STRENGTH	10
BRAINS	4
ATTACK	8
DEFENSE	7

THE SPLASHDOWN

The world's biggest snake meets one of the biggest freshwater fish in a contest of Amazonian giants. The green anaconda waits in ambush with only its eyes and nostrils above the water. The arapaima hunts near the surface, sometimes even snatching birds as prey.

ARAPAIMA

This huge fish is an air breather with a primitive lung. The arapaima surfaces about every ten minutes to gulp air with a loud coughing sound.

STATS

7	SPEED	
8	STRENGTH	
7	BRAINS	
7	ATTACK	
7	DEFENSE	

SCIENTIFIC NAME	*Arapaima gigas*
LENGTH	6–10 feet (1.8–3 m)
TYPICAL PREY	Fish, sometimes birds
PREDATOR STYLE	Hunts near the surface of the water
WATER TYPE	Fresh

WHO WINS? SEE PAGE 64.

GANGES RIVER DOLPHIN VS. GHARIAL

GANGES RIVER DOLPHIN

This endangered mammal is almost blind, but eyes aren't much use anyway in the muddy water where it lives. Instead, it "sees" with echolocation (sonar).

SCIENTIFIC NAME	*Platanista gangetica*
LENGTH	7–11.5 feet (2.1–3.5 m)
TYPICAL PREY	Bottom-dwelling crustaceans, mollusks, and fish
PREDATOR STYLE	Hunts by echolocation (sonar) along the river bottom
WATER TYPE	Fresh

STATS

SPEED	8
STRENGTH	7
BRAINS	9
ATTACK	5
DEFENSE	5

THE SPLASHDOWN

Two long-snouted river-dwellers from South Asia meet in this Indian splashdown. The Ganges River dolphin hunts fish, mollusks, and crustaceans in the muddy river that gives it its name. The gharial's narrow, toothy snout is built for whipping quickly sideways through the water.

GHARIAL

The gharial is one of the biggest members of the crocodile family. It's fast and agile in the water but a slow mover on land.

STATS

6	SPEED
8	STRENGTH
4	BRAINS
6	ATTACK
7	DEFENSE

SCIENTIFIC NAME	*Gavialis gangeticus*
LENGTH	13–20 feet (4–6.1 m)
TYPICAL PREY	Fish
PREDATOR STYLE	Ambush hunter; waits motionless in water, then whips snout sideways to snap up passing fish
WATER TYPE	Fresh

WHO WINS?
SEE PAGE 64.

BULL SHARK VS. ALLIGATOR GAR

BULL SHARK

This saltwater predator can travel long distances up freshwater rivers. Bull sharks have been found up to 2,500 miles (4,023 km) from the ocean.

SCIENTIFIC NAME	*Carcharhinus leucas*
LENGTH	7–11 feet (2.1–3.4 m)
TYPICAL PREY	Fish of all types, including stingrays and smaller sharks
PREDATOR STYLE	Hunts along the ocean and river bottoms, pursues prey with quick bursts of speed
WATER TYPE	Salt/Fresh

STATS	
SPEED	8
STRENGTH	8
BRAINS	6
ATTACK	9
DEFENSE	9

THE SPLASHDOWN

The saltwater bull shark travels up the river to face off against the alligator gar. The bull shark is one of the most dangerous sharks in the world to humans. Is the alligator gar as tough as it looks?

ALLIGATOR GAR

The alligator gar is one of the biggest freshwater fish in North America. It often floats like a log near the water's surface to ambush prey.

STATS

5	SPEED	
6	STRENGTH	
4	BRAINS	
6	ATTACK	
6	DEFENSE	

SCIENTIFIC NAME	*Atractosteus spatula*
LENGTH	6–10 feet (1.8–3 m)
TYPICAL PREY	Fish, crabs, sometimes birds
PREDATOR STYLE	Ambush hunter; floats motionless in wait for prey
WATER TYPE	Fresh

WHO WINS?
SEE PAGE 64.

COTTONMOUTH VS. ALLIGATOR SNAPPING TURTLE

COTTONMOUTH

The cottonmouth gets its name from the warning it gives when threatened: it opens its jaws to show off fangs and the white-colored lining of its mouth.

SCIENTIFIC NAME	*Agkistrodon piscivorus*
LENGTH	3–6 feet (91–183 cm)
TYPICAL PREY	Fish, amphibians, reptiles, birds, small mammals
PREDATOR STYLE	Subdues prey with venomous bite; detects warm-blooded prey with heat-sensing organs in its face
WATER TYPE	Fresh

STATS

SPEED	7
STRENGTH	5
BRAINS	4
ATTACK	8
DEFENSE	8

THE SPLASHDOWN

It's a splashdown in the swamp as these two North American reptiles face off. The venomous cottonmouth, or water moccasin, is a relative of the rattlesnake. The alligator snapping turtle is the largest freshwater turtle in the Americas.

ALLIGATOR SNAPPING TURTLE

This huge turtle opens its mouth underwater to show a bright pink, worm-shaped lure on its tongue. Any prey that comes close to investigate gets snapped up.

STATS

5	SPEED	
7	STRENGTH	
4	BRAINS	
6	ATTACK	
6	DEFENSE	

SCIENTIFIC NAME	*Macrochelys temminckii*
LENGTH	2–2.5 feet (61–76 cm) shell length
TYPICAL PREY	Fish, frogs, snakes, crayfish, other turtles, plants
PREDATOR STYLE	Attracts prey with lure in mouth
WATER TYPE	Fresh

WHO WINS?
SEE PAGE 64.

ELECTRIC EEL VS. RED-BELLIED PIRANHA

ELECTRIC EEL

The electric eel can deliver a zap of more than 600 volts. Nearly blind, it uses lower-voltage electrical signals to search for prey.

SCIENTIFIC NAME	*Electrophorus electricus*
LENGTH	6–8 feet (1.8–2.4 m)
TYPICAL PREY	Fish, amphibians, sometimes small birds and mammals
PREDATOR STYLE	Stuns prey with a powerful electric shock, then gulps it down
WATER TYPE	Fresh

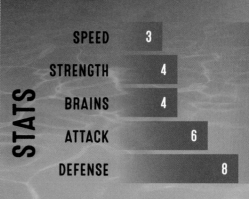

STATS

SPEED	3
STRENGTH	4
BRAINS	4
ATTACK	6
DEFENSE	8

THE SPLASHDOWN

The Amazonian eel packs a powerful zap, but is it strong enough to vanquish a pack of piranhas? Electric eels paralyze their prey with high-voltage shocks. Pack-hunting piranhas may have small mouths, but their jaws are powerful and their teeth are razor sharp.

RED-BELLIED PIRANHA

This razor-toothed fish has a deadly reputation, but it only preys on large animals (or humans) if they're sick, injured, or already dead.

STATS

5	SPEED
6	STRENGTH
5	BRAINS
8	ATTACK
7	DEFENSE

SCIENTIFIC NAME	*Pygocentrus nattereri*
LENGTH	10–14 inches (25–36 cm)
TYPICAL PREY	Fish, mollusks, insects, crustaceans, carrion, plants
PREDATOR STYLE	Pack hunter, feeds in groups on larger animals
WATER TYPE	Fresh

WHO WINS?
SEE PAGE 64.

BELOW THE SURFACE:
FRESH WATER

Only about 3 percent of the water on the surface of the earth is fresh water. But the animals that live and hunt there can be just as large and fearsome as saltwater predators.

Some of them also hunt in brackish water, which means water that is slightly salty. Brackish water is found in estuaries, where rivers meet the ocean.

These are some of the special weapons used by splashdown predators who live or hunt at least some of the time in freshwater streams, rivers, and lakes.

VENOMOUS SPURS

PLATYPUS

VENOMOUS STING

FRESHWATER STINGRAY

TEETH

CROCODILE

LURE ON TONGUE

ALLIGATOR SNAPPING TURTLE

VENOMOUS BITE

COTTONMOUTH

CONSTRICTING COILS

GREEN ANACONDA

GIANT OTTER VS. STINGRAY

GIANT OTTER

Giant otters live and often hunt together in family groups. This member of the weasel family can weigh in at as much as 75 lb (34 kg).

SCIENTIFIC NAME	*Pteronura brasiliensis*
LENGTH	5–6 feet (1.5–1.8 m)
TYPICAL PREY	Fish
PREDATOR STYLE	Hunts alone or in groups in the water near the banks of rivers, streams, and lakes
WATER TYPE	Fresh

STATS

SPEED	6
STRENGTH	6
BRAINS	8
ATTACK	7
DEFENSE	7

THE SPLASHDOWN

It's a South American splashdown as the world's longest otter faces off against a small, river-dwelling stingray. The otter is more than five times the size of the stingray, but the ray has a powerful secret weapon: its venomous sting!

SMOOTH-BACKED FRESHWATER STINGRAY

Like its saltwater cousins, this river-dwelling stingray defends itself with a barbed, venom-tipped spine near the base of its tail. The sting is painful but not deadly.

STATS

5	SPEED
3	STRENGTH
4	BRAINS
3	ATTACK
7	DEFENSE

SCIENTIFIC NAME	*Potamotrygon orbignyi*
LENGTH	9–15 inches (23–38 cm)
TYPICAL PREY	Water-dwelling insects and crustaceans
PREDATOR STYLE	Uses special sensor cells around its mouth to detect electrical charges from prey along the river bottom
WATER TYPE	Fresh

WHO WINS? SEE PAGE 64.

GOLIATH TIGER FISH VS. JAPANESE GIANT SALAMANDER

GOLIATH TIGER FISH

This toothy river dweller lurks in eddies and calm areas of whitewater rapids. When it spots a fish, it chases down its prey with a burst of speed.

SCIENTIFIC NAME	*Hydrocynus goliath*
LENGTH	4–5 feet (1.2–1.5 m)
TYPICAL PREY	Fish
PREDATOR STYLE	Ambush hunter
WATER TYPE	Fresh

STATS

SPEED	7
STRENGTH	7
BRAINS	4
ATTACK	7
DEFENSE	7

THE SPLASHDOWN

What if. . .? Predators from opposite sides of the world match fighting skills in a freshwater splashdown. The goliath tigerfish lives in Africa's Congo River Basin. The giant salamander, the world's second-largest amphibian, lives in the mountain streams of Japan.

JAPANESE GIANT SALAMANDER

This huge amphibian is nearly blind. It navigates and hunts in the water using its other senses, including special vibration-sensing cells in its skin.

STATS	
4	SPEED
5	STRENGTH
4	BRAINS
4	ATTACK
4	DEFENSE

SCIENTIFIC NAME	*Andrias japonicus*
LENGTH	5 feet (1.5 m)
TYPICAL PREY	Fish, insects, crustaceans, anything else it can catch
PREDATOR STYLE	Hunts using senses of smell, touch, and vibration-detecting cells in skin
WATER TYPE	Fresh

WHO WINS?
SEE PAGE 64.

NILE CROCODILE VS. HIPPOPOTAMUS

NILE CROCODILE

Nile crocodiles will hunt anything they can catch, including large mammals like zebras, wildebeests, and even humans. They can eat half their own weight in a single meal.

SCIENTIFIC NAME	*Crocodylus niloticus*
LENGTH	7–16 feet (2.1–4.9 m)
TYPICAL PREY	Mostly fish, also mammals, birds, and other crocodiles
PREDATOR STYLE	Ambush hunter; sometimes hunts in groups
WATER TYPE	Fresh

STATS

SPEED	6
STRENGTH	10
BRAINS	4
ATTACK	10
DEFENSE	10

THE SPLASHDOWN

Frequent foes face off in an African river battle. The Nile crocodile is the second-largest croc in the world. Its prey includes small hippos. The hippo may be a vegetarian, but it can defend itself in a fight with its enormous size and dagger-sharp canine teeth.

HIPPOPOTAMUS

Hippos spend the day in the water, where their huge bodies become graceful as they swim and walk along the river bottom. They graze at night.

STATS		
8	SPEED	
10	STRENGTH	
7	BRAINS	
8	ATTACK	
9	DEFENSE	

SCIENTIFIC NAME	*Hippopotamus amphibius*
LENGTH	9–16 feet (2.7–4.9 m)
TYPICAL PREY	Herbivorous; eats grass and other plants
PREDATOR STYLE	Grazes on land at night
WATER TYPE	Fresh

WHO WINS?
SEE PAGE 64.

PLATYPUS VS. NEEDLEFISH

PLATYPUS

The platypus is one of only two mammal types that lays eggs. Its body is built for swimming and digging in muddy lake and river bottoms.

SCIENTIFIC NAME	*Ornithorhynchus anatinus*
LENGTH	12–24 inches (30–61 cm)
TYPICAL PREY	Insects, mollusks, worms
PREDATOR STYLE	Forages for prey on river bottoms
WATER TYPE	Fresh

STATS

SPEED	4
STRENGTH	4
BRAINS	6
ATTACK	1
DEFENSE	7

THE SPLASHDOWN

What if . . . ? A freshwater mammal meets a saltwater fish in this contest between two strange-looking predators. Male platypuses defend themselves with venomous spurs on their hind legs. Needlefish beaks are needle sharp and can cause serious injury.

REEF NEEDLEFISH

These needlefish often make high-speed leaps out of the water as they swim near the surface. Humans have been injured and even killed by flying needlefish.

STATS	
9	SPEED
5	STRENGTH
4	BRAINS
2	ATTACK
6	DEFENSE

SCIENTIFIC NAME	*Strongylura incisa*
LENGTH	24–39 inches (61–99 cm)
TYPICAL PREY	Fish
PREDATOR STYLE	Hunts near the surface; uses jaws to snap up fish, does not use its beak to spear prey
WATER TYPE	Salt

WHO WINS?
SEE PAGE 64.

GIANT MORAY

One of the biggest moray eels, the giant moray prowls for prey among the cracks and crevices of its coral-reef home. It will attack humans if threatened.

SCIENTIFIC NAME	*Gymnothorax javanicus*
LENGTH	Up to 10 feet (3 m)
TYPICAL PREY	Fish, crustaceans
PREDATOR STYLE	Hunts in coral reefs
WATER TYPE	Salt

STATS

SPEED	5
STRENGTH	5
BRAINS	5
ATTACK	5
DEFENSE	5

THE SPLASHDOWN

What if . . . ? It's every eel for itself when the saltwater moray meets the river-dwelling longfin. The giant moray lives in shallow-water ocean reefs. The longfin eel spends its whole life in fresh water, then swims downstream to the ocean to spawn.

NEW ZEALAND LONGFIN EEL

This eel has a long life to match its long body. Some New Zealand longfin eels live more than 100 years.

STATS

5	SPEED	
4	STRENGTH	
3	BRAINS	
3	ATTACK	
3	DEFENSE	

SCIENTIFIC NAME	*Anguilla dieffenbachii*
LENGTH	2–5 feet (61–152 cm)
TYPICAL PREY	Fish, crustaceans
PREDATOR STYLE	Stalks prey among rocks and plants on river and lake bottoms
WATER TYPE	Fresh

WHO WINS?
SEE PAGE 64.

AMERICAN ALLIGATOR VS. SALTWATER CROCODILE

AMERICAN ALLIGATOR

This hunter has a champion chomp. A big alligator's jaws clamp down with 2,000 pounds (909 kg) of force, more than 16 times the biting power of a human.

SCIENTIFIC NAME	*Alligator mississippiensis*
LENGTH	8–15 feet (2.4–4.6 m)
TYPICAL PREY	Fish, turtles, snakes, small mammals, carrion
PREDATOR STYLE	Ambush hunter
WATER TYPE	Fresh

STATS

SPEED	6
STRENGTH	10
BRAINS	4
ATTACK	9
DEFENSE	9

THE SPLASHDOWN

What if . . . ? It's the ultimate crocodilian splashdown, with the toughest reptile of North America going up against the biggest croc of them all, from half a world away. Can the American hunter hold its own against the largest reptile in the world?

SALTWATER CROCODILE

Like other crocodilians, the "saltie" hunts by ambush, often lying in wait near the shore, then lunging out to drag large animals into the water.

STATS	
6	SPEED
10	STRENGTH
4	BRAINS
10	ATTACK
10	DEFENSE

SCIENTIFIC NAME	*Crocodylus porosus*
LENGTH	10–20 feet (3–6.1 m)
TYPICAL PREY	Anything it can catch, including fish, reptiles, and large mammals
PREDATOR STYLE	Ambush hunter
WATER TYPE	Salt/Fresh

WHO WINS?
SEE PAGE 64.

WHO WOULD WIN?

The experts pick their splashdown champions. Do you agree?

p. 6–7
BANDED SEA KRAIT VS. SEA SNAKE

The sea krait's larger size gives it the advantage, but the yellow-bellied sea snake can stay below the surface longer. The splashdown ends in a draw.

p. 8–9
BLUE MARLIN VS. SWORDFISH

Superior size and strength carry the day. The victory goes to the blue marlin.

p. 10–11
BLUE-RINGED OCTOPUS VS. REEF STONEFISH

The stonefish is larger, but its spines work only for defense, not attack. The tiny octopus wins the battle with its deadly bite.

p. 12–13
BLUEFIN TUNA VS. LIONFISH

The lionfish keeps to the crevices of its coral reef habitat, where the huge tuna can't follow. The lionfish's venomous sting sends the tuna on a hasty retreat.

p.14–15
NORTHERN STARGAZER VS. PACIFIC ELECTRIC RAY

Even though both opponents can produce a 50-volt zap, the electric ray packs more power into its jolts. The victory goes to the ray.

p. 16–17
GIANT PACIFIC OCTOPUS VS. HARBOR SEAL

In an underwater wrestling match, the seal barely escapes from the octopus's powerful grip in time to reach the surface to breathe. The octopus is the winner.

p. 18–19
GREAT BARRACUDA VS. GRAY REEF SHARK

Size, power, and aggressiveness triumph over speed in this contest. The shark is the winner.

p. 20–21
GREAT HAMMERHEAD VS. LEMON SHARK

The lemon shark puts up a good fight, but in the end it is no match for the larger, agile hammerhead. The great hammerhead is victorious.

p. 24–25
ORCA VS. GREAT WHITE SHARK

In a ferocious battle, the killer whale finally gets the upper hand. The orca wins the splashdown.

p. 26–27
POLAR BEAR VS. WALRUS

The bear charges, but the walrus flops into the water just in time. The bear is a good swimmer, but the walrus can dive deeper and stay under longer. The contest is a tie.

p. 28–29
BALLOONFISH VS. OYSTER TOADFISH

With its opponent puffed out like a prickly balloon, the toadfish can't get past the spines for a bite. The contest goes to the pufferfish.

p. 30–31
PORTUGUESE MAN-OF-WAR VS. AUSTRALIAN BOX JELLYFISH

The box jellyfish can swim, while the man-of-war can only drift with the wind and currents. The more maneuverable box jellyfish is victorious.

p. 32–33
SPERM WHALE VS. GIANT SQUID

The squid puts up a ferocious fight, but the whale's peg-toothed jaw stays clamped on the mollusk's body. The whale gets a squid dinner.

p. 36–37
ANGLERFISH VS. PELICAN EEL

Glowing lures work best when the prey is smaller than the predator. The gulper eel zeroes in on the anglerfish's lure and swallows its opponent with a single gulp.

p. 38–39
PACIFIC BLACKDRAGON VS. FRILLED SHARK

The blackdragon has the speed, but it doesn't have a big enough mouth to cause much harm to the shark. The battle ends in a draw.

p. 40–41
GREEN ANACONDA VS. ARAPAIMA

The lurking anaconda grabs the arapaima when it surfaces to breathe. The fish succumbs to the unyielding grip of the snake's squeezing coils.

p. 42–43
GANGES RIVER DOLPHIN VS. GHARIAL

The gharial's motionless ambush method doesn't fool the dolphin's sonar sense. Victory goes to the dolphin.

p. 44–45
BULL SHARK VS. ALLIGATOR GAR

The alligator gar can't get the better of the faster, heavier bull shark. The shark wins the splashdown.

p. 46–47
COTTONMOUTH VS. ALLIGATOR SNAPPING TURTLE

The turtle pulls into its shell to protect itself. When the snake's strike misses, the turtle wins the contest with one snapping chomp.

p. 48–49
ELECTRIC EEL VS. RED-BELLIED PIRANHA

The electric eel zaps the whole pack of piranhas at the same time. The showdown is over in moments, with the eel victorious.

p. 52–53
GIANT OTTER VS. STINGRAY

The otter dives in for a direct attack, only to get a jab from the stingray's venomous barb. The otter retreats in pain, and the ray wins the day.

p. 54–55
GOLIATH TIGERFISH VS. JAPANESE GIANT SALAMANDER

The nearly sightless salamander can't keep up with the sharp-eyed tigerfish. The victory goes to the tigerfish.

p. 56–57
NILE CROCODILE VS. HIPPOPOTAMUS

Even the biggest crocodile has a hard time standing up to a full-grown hippo. The hippopotamus wins with a tank-like charge and a hippo-sized chomp.

p. 58–59
PLATYPUS VS. NEEDLEFISH

The needlefish snaps with its jaws but doesn't use its beak as an offensive stabbing weapon. The platypus's venomous spurs give it the edge in the fight. The platypus wins.

p. 60–61
GIANT MORAY VS. LONGFIN EEL

In spite of the giant moray's fiercer looks, these two are about as evenly matched as a pair of eels from different habitats can be. The contest ends in a tie.

p. 62–63
AMERICAN ALLIGATOR VS. SALTWATER CROCODILE

In this brute-force contest, size and weight make all the difference. The croc wins the splashdown by a chomp!